Handbook for Winning Jehovah's Witnesses to Christ

By Dr. Bill Bennett

Handbook for Winning Jehovah's Witnesses to Christ
Copyright © 2012

All Rights Reserved.
No part of this book may be reproduced in any form without permission in writing from the author or publisher.

ISBN: 978-1-935256-27-4

Ledge Press
PO Box 1652
Boone, NC 28607
ledgepress.com
ledgepress@gmail.com

FOREWORD

Before making this intense study of the Jehovah Witnesses, I admit that I held the wrong attitude toward them, believing they were mean-spirited, even hateful, deceivers and evil fanatical propagators of devastating false teaching.

However, after I researched the history and practices of the Jehovah Witnesses, I discovered that they are not primarily deceivers themselves, but have been deceived by their deceived leaders. Therefore, our witness to Jehovah Witnesses should be marked by full understanding, even great compassion, patience, and the highest concern for the salvation of their immortal souls.

In light of my observation above, I am moved to dedicate this book to my precious wife of 58 years, Doris (promoted to heaven, October 29, 2010), who possessed enormous compassion for all the lost, including the Jehovah Witnesses.

I. Why Study The Jehovah's Witnesses?

Have you ever had this experience? You probably have. If not, you most certainly will. Two people come to your door carrying a bag containing some literature which seems to be interesting and very innocent. They offer to sell you their literature and begin to talk to you about Jehovah, God, and about his Kingdom. Suddenly, if you have not realized it before, you recognize that these are Jehovah's Witnesses.

You have heard about the Witnesses, but you may not know who they really are or what they actually believe. You probably do one of two things, both of which are wrong. You may just tell them you are not interested and then slam the door in their faces. Or, perhaps you invite them in, either out of curiosity or out of a desire to "discuss" ("argue" may be a better term) doctrine with them. If you have done either of these two things, you have violated 1 Peter 3:15, "But in your hearts set Christ as Lord. Always be prepared to give answer to everyone who asks you to give the reason for the hope that you have. But do this with gentleness and respect."

This verse of Scripture tells us exactly why we should study the Jehovah's Witnesses. First, by studying them, we are able to set apart Christ as Lord. In studying what the Witnesses believe, we must, out of necessity, study what we believe, using the Bible as our main text book. In so doing, we set Christ apart as Lord, knowing that He is the Son of

God, God Incarnate, the risen, reigning Savior of the world. It is He alone who is Lord, nobody else. We are saved solely by faith in Him. Second, we are able to give an answer for the hope that we have. The problem with many Christians who confront Jehovah's Witnesses is that we confront them unprepared; unable to give answers for what we believe and unable to answer their false claims with the truth of God's Word. We must know what we believe and why we believe it before we can be prepared to confront the Witnesses. We must know what they believe, why it is wrong, and how it contradicts the truth of the Bible. Third, we are able to confront Witnesses with gentleness and respect when we are adequately prepared to confront them. A person who is not prepared to discuss anything intelligently will often resort to arguing, usually lacking gentleness and respect. Such a person often makes a fool of himself and accomplishes nothing.

We do not study Jehovah's Witnesses in order to attack them, nor do we want to put them down. If these are our motives, then we are being neither Christian nor biblical in our approach. No, instead we ought to love them. We want to teach them, reach them, and lead them to the saving grace of our Lord Jesus Christ. What a joy it will be to hear a Witness say, "Jesus is Lord" simply because we took time to learn about him, care about him, and rescue him from falsehood.

II. Jesus Died For Witnesses Too!

The problem with many Christians in dealing with Witnesses is that we are often burdened by them rather than burdened for them. There is a difference! We often allow them to burden us with their zeal, persistence, and determination. We find it easier to shut them out rather than invite them into our lives, and we thereby fail to share Christ with them. What a shame! What a sin! We must accept the fact that Jesus died for Witnesses too. With that understanding, we must also accept the fact that we are responsible for doing everything possible to win as many Witnesses as we can.

Who are these Witnesses? They are not deceivers; they are deceived. Satan is the great deceiver of many, and certainly many have been deceived by him. Yet, if we survey the great vastness of God's love, we find enormous portions of grace reserved for our friends, the Jehovah's Witnesses. Who are they? They are precious souls for whom our Lord Jesus died. They are among those whom Jesus has commanded us to reach for Him. They are our responsibility. Will we be burdened by them or will we be burdened for them? They eagerly seek to reach you. Will you eagerly seek to reach them?

III. The Origin of the Jehovah's Witnesses

The founder of the Jehovah's Witnesses organization was Charles Taze Russell, who lived from 1852-1916. Reared in Alleghany, Pennsylvania, Russell was indoctrinated with the teachings of the Congregational Church. He began to doubt some of their basic doctrines, especially eternal punishment, and later became involved in the teachings of the Seventh-Day Adventists. In 1870, he began to teach a Bible study of which he was elected "Pastor" in 1876. In this Bible study, he rejected historical Christian doctrines including the Trinity, the deity of Christ, Christ's physical resurrection and physical second coming, and the eternal retribution for sin.

During these early years, Russell began to write and publish books and pamphlets. His favorite topics were his false views of hell and the second coming of Christ. He founded *The Herald of the Morning* publication, known today as *The Watchtower*. The publication has now reached 21 million copies per month in 78 languages. Another periodical, *Awake!*, has a circulation of 16 million copies per month in 67 languages.[1]

Russell had his share of problems in his life. He had marital problems, allegedly consisting of adulterous encounters, and was sued for divorce by his wife. The High Court of Ontario granted the divorce on the grounds of "his conceit, egotism, domination, and improper conduct in relation

---
[1] Walter Martin, *The Rise of the Cults*, (Santa Anna, CA: Vision House, 1980) p. 20.

to other women." [2] He was also found to be guilty of perjuring himself in court and of other fraudulent activities.[3] Van Baalen's words are strong, yet true, "There is a reciprocity between a man's character and his theology. St. Paul teaches in Romans 9:19-20 that bad theology proceeds from a bad heart."[4]

Most Jehovah's Witnesses disclaim any connection with Russell, who died in 1916, yet it is obvious that he was the founder of the movement and that many of his teachings make up the now existing doctrine of the cult. He established their headquarters in Brooklyn and founded the "Zion Watchtower Tract Society" in 1884. He published seven books, including *The Millennial Dawn* and *Studies in the Scriptures* from which many of the movement's doctrines developed. After his death, he was followed by J. F. "Judge" Rutherford, Nathan Homer Knox, and the present controller, Fredrick W. Franz, who have carried on the teachings of Russell.

---

[2] Anthony A. Hoekema, *The Four Major Cults*, (Grand Rapids: Eerdmans, 1976) p. 227.

[3] Kenneth Boa, *Cults, World Religions And The Occult*, (Wheaton: Victor, 1990), 97. Boa reports "He (Russell) was charged with fraudulent activities by the 'Brooklyn Daily Eagle' and clearly perjured himself in court. Under oath he testified that he knew the Greek alphabet, but when he was unable to identify the letters of the alphabet on request, he was forced to retract. For a further discussion of the legal difficulties of Russell, see Martin, *The Kingdom of the Cults*, pp. 38-47.

[4] J. K. Van Baalen, *The Chaos of Cults*, (Grand Rapids: Eerdmans, 1975). P. 259

IV. A Challenge to Christianity

The Jehovah's Witnesses are a challenge to Christianity for several reasons. First, they are a growing movement. Though the cult began in 1884, most of its growth has taken place in the past 15-20 years, and it will probably continue to increase in numbers and strength through evangelism and publishing. Though only one of every 740 house calls produces a member, they increase by about 200,000 members per year. The movement grew by 45% during the 1970's. In 1985 alone, members spent 590,540,205 hours in world-wide missionary outreach, equivalent to almost 67,500 years.[5] They published 100,000 books and 800,000 copies of their two magazines daily.[6]

Second, the Witnesses teach false doctrines that are in opposition to historical Christianity. They believe that the Christian church is of the devil. Their teachings deny essential Christian doctrines, including the deity of Christ, the person and work of the Holy Spirit, and the existence of hell. The Witnesses claim that their teachings are the only truth about the Bible.

Third, the Witnesses have misrepresented the authority of the Christian church, the Bible. The Jehovah's Witnesses have their own version of the Bible. *The New World Translation of Holy Scripture*, of which the translators are anonymous

---

[5] Bob Larson, *Larson's New Book of Cults*, (Wheaton: Tyndale House, 1982), p. 270

[6] Ibid. p. 269.

and their credentials cannot be checked. This version differs greatly and significantly from other translations of the Bible.[7] It is seen by the Witnesses to be the only true and authoritative translation of Scripture. In spite of their repeated appeal to Scripture as the inspired message from God, they place reason above the Bible and reject that in the Bible which is contrary to reason.

Fourth, the Witnesses seem driven to outwork the normal Christian. With the zealous missionary efforts of the Witnesses, they are very active in spreading

---

[7] One of the most significant differences in the *New World Translation* is found in John 1:1. They render the phrase "the Word was God" (KJV) as "the Word was a god." Tucker says, "Their argument is that in the Greek there is a definite article used for God (Ton Theon) with the phrase, 'the Word was with God,' thus indicating that 'God' is referring to Jehovah. In the following phrase, 'the Word was God,' however, there is no definite article for God (Theos), thus showing a divine being inferior to Jehovah."

Ruth A. Tucker, *Another Gospel*, (Grand Rapids: Zondervan, 1989). P. 139.

But anyone who knows Greek realizes that this is a clear mistranslation. The subject of the sentence is HO LOGOS or "The Word," which is made plain by the definite article ("The") preceeding the subject "Word"). The predicate is "God" or THEOS, and it has no article preceeding it meaning it cannot be translated "a god." The correct translation is very clear. "The Word was God." This shows plainly that the Bible does call Jesus "God," disproving *The Watchtower*'s notion that He is inferior to God.

One can see from this example how the Jehovah's Witnesses have mistranslated the Scriptures to support their false doctrines. It is suggested that one study carefully the many other mistranslation found in *The New World Translation* and how these translations effect theological positions.

The Watchtower's false doctrines. In their efforts to evangelize the world, they are not motivated by love for people or for God, but rather, they are driven by a dreadful fear of annihilation of the soul and body. They witness in order to be saved. In fact, Jehovah Witnesses have a bitter hatred for Christianity and relish the idea of all Christians being destroyed at Armageddon. When one tries to convert a Christian to Jehovah's Witness belief, it is not out of love, but out of a selfish desire for eternal hope.

Indeed, the Jehovah's Witnesses do pose a challenge to Christianity. With their rapid growth and increasing strength, they seem to excel where many Christian churches and denominations are falling behind. Basic and unifying Christian doctrines are being denied by *The Watchtower* and their false doctrines are being spread. Even the authority with which we are identified, the Bible, is being misinterpreted and misrepresented by the Witnesses.

V. A False System of Doctrine

DOCTRINE OF GOD
The Jehovah's Witnesses deny the Trinity: the Father, Son and the Holy Spirit–the three being one God. They say that only Jehovah is God. He is one solitary being, the sole Creator and Preserver of the universe. They deny the deity of Jesus and say that the Holy Spirit is not personal, but rather is an impersonal active force of God. The doctrine of the Trinity, they claim, is a creation of Satan. However, the Bible teaches that God is an eternal, personal being in three-persons – the Father, Son and the Holy Spirit (Matthew 3:13-17; 28:19; II Cor. 13-14).

DOCTRINE OF JESUS CHRIST
The Witnesses flatly deny the deity of Christ. They claim that Christ was the first of God's creations, but He is not the Creator of all things. He is not God; rather He is a god, unequal to Jehovah. The Witnesses further describe Christ as a mighty god, but not the God almighty who is Jehovah, and that while He was on earth He was stripped of any and all deity. In fact, they claim that He was the incarnation of Michael the Archangel. He was an example of human perfection in response to Jehovah's moral law. His death did not atone for man's sin, for only Jehovah can save. Christ's death only provided man an opportunity to work for his salvation. There was no physical resurrection, but Christ arose from the grave only as a spirit person. The return of Christ is only a spiritual one since He has no physical body. In fact, according to

Witnesses' belief, He returned in 1914, and in 1918 He came to His temple to head the body of the church who are the 144,000.

However, the Bible teaches us differently concerning our Lord Jesus Christ. Christ is deity, a part of the Trinity, God Himself (John 1:1; Colossians 1:15-19, 2:9; 1 John 5:7-8). Christ was bodily resurrected from the grave (John 2:21, 20:24-29); Luke 24:36-43). Christ will return physically (1 Thessalonians 4:16-17; Matthew 24:30; Zechariah 12:10; Revelation 1:7).

DOCTRINE OF MAN

Jehovah's Witnesses claim that man's soul is inseparable from the body. Man is a soul; he does not simply have a soul. When a man dies, his body and soul together cease to exist. Immortality of the soul is a doctrine created by Satan. Man is recreated by God after death from the memory of Jehovah. The recreated ones are the persons who will inhabit the kingdom. However, the Bible teaches that man has an eternal, immortal soul (Genesis 1:26, 5:1; Job 32:8; Acts 7:59; 1 Corinthians 11:7).

DOCTRINE OF SALVATION

This is the worst false doctrine the Witnesses have. They claim that Christ's death does not atone for sin. His death does not purchase forgiveness of sin nor entrance into Heaven, but it purchased earthly life and blessings lost by Adam's sin. Christ's death only provides an opportunity for eternal life through pleasing Jehovah with good works. His death applies only to the 144,000 elite group of Jehovah's Witnesses. Salvation is earned through good works. These works include studying the Bible (only *The New World Translation*), associating with Jehovah's Witnesses, changing from worldly ways through Jehovah's

Witnesses baptism, and being a witness (evangelists) of God's kingdom. Man is saved into the kingdom, not saved from hell. 144,000 will reign in heaven with Jesus. The "other sheep" will have an earthly, Eden-like paradise while all others will be in "soul-sleep" for 1,000 years waiting recreation. There is no hell. There is a second chance after death. Jehovah will recreate all who never knew about Him. Those who knew about but rejected Jehovah in the first life will be annihilated. The recreated will be educated for 1,000 years, and after that time, the judgment day will come and the recreated will either reject Jehovah and be annihilated or accept Him and live forever on earth.

The Bible knows nothing of any of this. Christ's death was the complete payment for man's sin (Romans 3:24-25; Colossians 1:20; 1 Peter 2:24;II Corinthians 5:20). One is saved through faith by Christ alone, not by any works (Ephesians 2:8-9; Titus 3:5; John 3:16). All who are saved by Christ through faith enter one heaven (John 14:1-3; Revelation 21:22). There is eternal punishment for sin, which is hell, for all who reject salvation from Christ through faith (Matthew 5:22; 8:11-12, 13:42, 50; Luke 13:24-28; II Peter 2:17; Jude 13; Revelation 14:9-11).

VI. Reaching The Witnesses

Have you ever gone on a road trip to a place you have never ventured to before? I did so once and I thought I knew where I was going. So, I set out on my trip with no preparation. Not too far down the road I realized I was going in the wrong direction. So, I went another direction. Still, I was not right. I tried several other roads, but the more I traveled, the more confused and lost I became. Because I had failed to prepare, I had no direction and I never reached my destination.

Such is the case for many Christians who venture to win a Witness to Christ. Many who travel this road find it to be unfamiliar territory though they are absolutely certain that they know how to reach their destination. If they travel down "Doctrine Drive," or "Apologetics Avenue," they are sure they will arrive at "Witness Winning Way." Yet, they find themselves lost and confused because they failed to prepare for their trip.

In order to win Jehovah's Witnesses, we must prepare ourselves for the task. There must be a solid game plan produced by much study and prayer. Robert A. Morey, in his little book, *How to Answer A Jehovah Witness*, offers us some good advice for the preparation of our game plan.[8] In his plan, he presents four main principles for witnessing to a Witness.

1. Recognize that the real problem in witnessing to a Jehovah's Witness is the question of authority. Jehovah's Witnesses believe that *The Watchtower* has the greatest and only genuine theologians and Bible experts existing today. They claim to have the best Greek and Hebrew translators of Scripture, while the fact remains that their writers are anonymous and therefore no credentials are available to be checked. The Bible as "correctly interpreted by *The Watchtower*" has exclusive authority, and no other religious books are to be read. To question the teachings or authority of *The Watchtower* is to risk being disfellowshipped. All religious issues are solved at the Jehovah's Witness headquarters in Brooklyn and nowhere else can truth be found. A Witness is trained not to trust himself nor others to interpret the Bible or to act as an authority on religion.

   A Christian, according to *The Watchtower*, has no religious authority, nor does the Christian Bible. In fact,

---

[8] Robert A. Morey, *How To Answer A Jehovah's Witness*, (Minneapolis: Bethany, 1980), pp. 13-17. Morey says, "An addeded incentive for your understanding this work is that the average church member wants his pastor or other church leaders to train him on how to handle the Jehovah's Witnesses who come knocking on their door. He is tired of simply shutting the door on Witnesses. He feels that he should be able to say something to defend his faith. Simply telling lay people not to talk to Jehovah's Witnesses gives credence to *The Watchtower* assertion that their arguments are unanswerable. Church members need and desire training." (p.13).

both the Christian and the Christian Bible are believed to be products of Satan. The Christian is Satan's child and the Bible was written by Satan to confuse and deceive people. The Bible has no authority and Christians are supposedly misled by regarding it as their primary authority. Therefore, the first step one must take in confronting a Witness is to understand the significance of the question of their authority.

2. To destroy the blind obedience and submission which the Jehovah's Witness has toward *The Watchtower*, one must demonstrate that the *The Watchtower* is not trustworthy or reliable. You must prove that it is not "God's visible organization on earth." The Witnesses' belief, trust, and confidence in *The Watchtower* must be undercut. He must be shown that he has been deceived and that *The Watchtower* is not God's religious authority on earth. Until his confidence in *The Watchtower* is destroyed, he cannot be led away from Jehovah Witness doctrines. He must trust God's Word alone. The only way we can gain common ground theologically is by establishing common authority. Until this happens, we cannot proceed in witnessing.

3. Destroy the Witnesses' blind allegiance to *The Watchtower* by showing from Scripture and official *Watchtower* literature that it is a false prophet. Since it is a false prophet, it is unreliable and not worthy of trust, respect, obedience or submission. Use the following five steps to establish this fact.

Step 1.
Establish from Scripture that if someone claims to be a prophet of God, the success or failure of their prophecies will determine whether they are a true or false prophet and

whether or not they speak in Yahweh's name. A false prophet will give false prophecies which do not come to pass. A true prophet of God will always be infallible in his prophecies. He will be right 100% of the time (Deuteronomy 18:20-22; Matthew 7:15-20). *The Watchtower* has claimed to be God's inspired prophet, who gives prophecies under angelic direction.

Step 2.
Deuteronomy 18:20-22 and Matthew 7:15-20 tell us how to judge whether or not *The Watchtower* is a true or false prophet and whether it truly speaks in Yahweh's name.

Step 3.
In 100 years of giving prophecies, there has been a 100% failure rate. All the prophecies of *The Watchtower* have been shown to be false by the passage of time. Time is a false prophet's worst enemy.

Step 4.
According to Deuteronomy 18 and Matthew 7, *The Watchtower* is a false prophet and does not speak in Yahweh's name. The Scriptures command us not to fear, respect, believe or trust *The Watchtower*.

Step 5.
Just as *The Watchtower* has been false in its prophecies, it is also false in its doctrines. *The Watchtower* has tried to cover up its false prophecies by willful and deliberate deceit and lies.

4. By the above method, you will be able to shatter the average Witness's confidence in *The Watchtower* as God's only channel of truth today. As you do this, be

sure to observe the following rules. First, always place the Witness on your side in the discussion. Tell him that *The Watchtower* is an organization that wants to deceive both of you. Stress that the Witness is not a false prophet himself, but he is someone who has been deceived by the false prophet, *The Watchtower*. Use the language like "we" to describe you and the Witness, and "they" when referring to *The Watchtower*.

Secondly, discuss and do not argue. Never argue doctrine or Biblical passages. Instead, simply lead the Witness to absolutely deny the authority of *The Watchtower* and to have complete confidence in the Bible as the source of authority. After doing so, you can reveal the error of the Witness's way and share with gentleness and respect the gospel of the Lord Jesus Christ.

VII. Rending Roots, Removing Leaves, Remaking Plants

There are two methods of removing leaves from a plant. First, you can remove each leaf by simply and tediously picking each one off, one at a time, until all of them have been removed and the plant has been stripped bare. Or, you can cut away the roots of the plant, never actually touching the leaves themselves; removing the plant's source of water, nutrition and life. Before long, the plant will die and nature herself will remove the leaves, leaving the plant bare.

In the first method, there is little more than a temporary removal of the leaves because life remains in the plant. You may strip it clean for a while, but as long as the roots remain giving food and life to the plant, the leaves will soon grow back again. In the second method, however, there is a permanent removal of the leaves. The work is not done upon the leaves, but rather upon the roots. It is the natural order of things which cause the leaves to fall, never to return. The plant dies without its roots and the leaves are unable to come forth again.

The "plant" in this illustration represents a Jehovah's Witness with his "roots" of authority (which consist of the teachings of *The Watchtower*) and his "leaves" of doctrine. How can we effectively lead a Witness to the truth of the Gospel? Many have tried to pick away at the "leaves", one at a time, arguing doctrine, hoping to strip the "plant" bare, while all the time the "plant" continued to live because the "roots" were not removed. Even if some of the "leaves" begin to wilt or fall because of doubts which arise in the Witnesses' system of belief as a result of the picking away at his doctrine, they will soon be restored if the "roots" which feed them are not removed.

If we are to strip a Witness of his false doctrine, we must accomplish it by rending, cutting away his religious authority that continues to feed him the poisonous waters of falsehood. We must deal with his authority, *The Watchtower*, not with his false doctrine. We must rent the "roots," allow the natural order of things to remove the "leaves" when the "plant" no longer has life, and watch God remake the "plant." When the "roots" are gone, the "leaves" will fall, never to return again. The "plant" will die.

Yes, the "plant" will die. The Jehovah's Witness will die when he confesses that *The Watchtower* is indeed a false prophet. Destroy *The Watchtower* and you destroy the Witnesses' doctrines. Destroy their doctrines and you destroy the Witness. The "roots," the "leaves," and the "plant" are gone. When the Witness dies, he must confess "Jesus is Lord," and with that confession, he is given life again. He becomes a "plant" made new. His "roots" of authority become the Word of God, which cannot err and which draws living water, nutrition, and life from the very being of God. His "leaves" of doctrines are given life from the "roots," and the new plant is beautifully adorned with them. The "plant" has been recreated and lives forever because its "roots" shall never pass away.

VIII. Handle With Care

We can witness to a Jehovah's Witness effectively only when we treat him or her appropriately. Just as God dealt with us lovingly and graciously while we were yet sinners, so must we lovingly and graciously deal with the Witnesses. There is no reason, nor is there any room, for rudeness, cruelty, disrespect, harshness, insensitivity, or any lack of love and grace when we confront them with the true Gospel of our Lord Jesus. In doing this, it will be helpful for you to keep the following items in mind.

1. Have the right attitude toward the Witness. Remember that *The Watchtower*, as an organization, is the enemy, not the Witness as an individual. These are people just like you. They have feelings and they can be hurt to the point that they will no longer listen to a Christian if dealt with improperly. You can be respectful, gentle, and firm at the same time. Keep in mind that a Christian has no right to be hostile toward a Witness. You should think negatively about the falsehoods of *The Watchtower*, but you must always think positively about the Witness as a person for whom our Lord gave His life. Your attitude may well determine your success as a light that shines in the darkness.

2. Have a love for his soul. Remember that he desperately needs to be redeemed. Express your love for his soul by communicating your concern and reservations for his false beliefs. Tell the Witness that you realize that

he is sincere in what he believes, but show him that he is sincerely wrong. Face him with the implications of his false beliefs in such a way that he understands your concern for his redemption, not in a way in which he feels condemned.

3. Tact and patience always pay dividends. Never overpower a Witness with religious clichés or blunt denunciations. Handle the conversation in such a way that he knows that what you're discussing is important to you. You are not there to win an argument, but to win a soul. Pray that the Lord gives you grace to out work, out pray, and out evangelize in Christian love those who are under the yoke of *The Watchtower*. As you speak to them from your head, be praying for them from your heart.

IX. Steps to Dealing With A Witness

In his short and helpful book, *Confronting Popular Cults*, Thomas Starkes offers some practical steps for dealing with a Jehovah's Witness.[9] The following procedure is recommended for evangelical Christians when they are confronted at their front door by a Witness.

1. Greet the visitor courteously. Give your name and ask his name. Ask if he lives in the neighborhood. Invite him in for a few minutes.

2. Indicate an appreciation for his zeal in spreading his faith and his interest in matters of religion.

3. Allow him to go through his first ten-minute presentation of what the Witnesses are emphasizing that particular month.

4. Buy any literature he has. He has paid for it out of his own pocket.

5. Ask leading questions which allow the Witness to affirm his own faith. An example is, "What has being a Jehovah's Witness done for your family?"

6. Give positive testimony of faith in Christ, stressing peace and joy in the life of a Christian disciple.

---

[9] M. Thomas Starkes, *Confronting Popular Cults*, (Nashville: Broadman, 1972), pp. 41-42.

7. To merely win the first argument with the Jehovah's Witness is often to lose him. Close off this first interview in about twenty minutes.

8. Plan quick follow-up action. The best procedure is to go see the Witness the very same day. This will allow him to see that his zeal in witnessing has been matched. It is good at this point to give the Witness a copy of *Good News for Modern Man*. Introduction of a new translation will allow some new thoughts to flow through the continuing conversation.

X. Conclusion - Are You Prepared?

Now that you have read this booklet, you may be asking yourself, "Am I now prepared to confront a Jehovah's Witness?" The answer is probably, "No, you are not." Why? For one thing, what you have just read is but a short overview–an introduction–to the world of *The Watchtower*. The purpose of this short work is to prompt you to greater concern and interest in this vast subject. It is hoped that this purpose has been served.

It has been said that there is none so dangerous as one who knows a little about everything and not much about anything. This is certainly true of a Christian who wishes to witness to a Jehovah's Witness. A little knowledge can do a lot of damage. You must be as prepared as possible before you seek to confront a Witness. Therefore, the following things are recommended.

1. Study books on Jehovah's Witnesses. You may want to begin with a book on cults in general, which has a single chapter on Jehovah's Witnesses. As you begin to learn more, you may then want to move to deeper and more complete studies. A bibliography can be found at the end of this booklet.

2. Memorize important names and dates from *Watchtower* history. This will give you a historical perspective on the subject and will make it obvious

that you are well versed in it. A list of dates has been added in Appendix A.

3. Know how *The Watchtower* doctrines differ from that which is taught in the Bible and in historical Christianity. You will find very significant differences in doctrines including God, Christ, man, immortality, atonement, and eschatology. A more complete section on these differences can be found in Appendix B.

4. Be familiar with terms used by Jehovah's Witnesses. If there is a communication problem because of unfamiliar terms, witnessing may become difficult. See Appendix C for a list of important terms.

5. Rehearse your knowledge of Jehovah's Witnesses by sharing it with fellow Christians.

You may do this during normal conversations or by teaching a Bible study on the subject to a small group. Never try to give the appearance of being an expert, but rather let them know that you are also in the process of learning. By rehearsing in this way, you are both preparing yourself for a witnessing experience and helping others learn about *The Watchtower*.

By following these five steps, you will become better prepared for witnessing to those who are in the clutches of *The Watchtower*. Continue to study. Continue to pray. Continue to care. Continue in the faith.

Appendix A

IMPORTANT DATES

1852 Birth of Charles Taze Russell in Allegheny, Pennsylvania.
1874 Russell elected Pastor of a Bible Study group and marked beginning of the cult - year of Russell's first prediction of Christ's return.
1879 First publication of Zion's Watch Tower and Herald of Christ's Presence.
1880 Thirty new congregations established in seven states.
1881 Zion's Watch Tower and Tract Society was established.
1884 Society was chartered and Jehovah Witness movement became official.
1914 Believed year of Christ's spiritual return; Russell's Armageddon prediction fails.
1915 Russell's second Armageddon prediction fails.
1916 Russell died and was succeeded by Joseph "Judge" Rutherford.
1918 Rutherford's first Armageddon prediction fails.
1925 Rutherford's second Armageddon prediction fails.
1931 Name "Jehovah Witnesses" adopted.
1942 Rutherford died and was followed by Nathan Homer Knorr.
1961 New World Translation of the Holy Scriptures published.
1975 Knorr's Armageddon prediction fails.

1977   Fred Franz assumes control of Jehovah Witnesses.
1986   Watch Tower circulation grows to 11,680,000 copies per issue.

Appendix B

DIFFERENCES BETWEEN JEHOVAH'S WITNESS AND CHRISTIAN DOCTRINE

GOD

CHRISTIANS:	JEHOVAH'S WITNESS:
God is eternal, personal, spiritual Being in three persons – the Trinity; Father, Son and Holy Sprit. (Matthew 3:13-17, 28:19; II Cor. 13:14).	There is one solitary being from all eternity, Jehovah God, the Creator and Preserver of the Universe and all things. They deny the doctrine Trinity.

IMMORTALITY

CHRISTIANS:	JEHOVAH'S WITNESS:
Scripture teaches that man has an Eternal, immortal soul (Genesis 1:26, 5:1; Job 32:8; Acts 7:59; I Cor. 11:17).	Man does not have an immortal soul. They teach that the soul is not separate from the body.

JESUS CHRIST

CHRISTIANS:	JEHOVAH'S WITNESS:
Christ is divine, a part of the Trinity, God Himself (John 1:1; Col. 1:15-19, 2:9; 1 John 5:7-8)	Christ was not God, but God's first created creature. They deny Christ's deity.

ATONEMENT

CHRISTIANS:	JEHOVAH'S WITNESS:
Christ's death was the complete payment For man's sins (Romans 3:24-25; Col. 1:20; I Peter 2:24; II Cor. 5:20)	Christ's death provides the opportunity for man to work for his salvation: perfect human life for eternity on an Eden-like earth.

CHRIST'S RESURRECTION

CHRISTIANS:	JEHOVAH'S WITNESS:
Christ was bodily resurrected from the Grave (John 2:21, 20:24-29; Luke 24:36-43).	Christ was raised a "divine spirit." They deny the bodily resurrection of Christ.

CHRIST'S RETURN

CHRISTIANS:	JEHOVAH'S WITNESS:
Christ will return to earth physically (I Thess. 4:16-17; Matthew 24:30; Zech. 12:10; Rev. 1:7).	Christ returned to earth – invisibly – in 1914 and now rules earth from heaven.

HELL

CHRISTIANS:	JEHOVAH'S WITNESS:
There is eternal punishment for sin (Matt. 5:22, 8:11:12, 13:42,50, 22:13; Luke 13:24-28; II Peter 2:17; Jude 13; Rev. 14:9-11).	There is no hell or eternal punishment. Those who do not measure up to Jehovah's standards will be annihilated, meaning they will be or know no more.

SALVATION

CHRISTIANS:	JEHOVAH'S WITNESS:
One is saved by Christ alone through Faith, not by works (Eph. 2:8-9; Titus 3:5; John 3:16).	One is saved by hard work. This accounts for "ardent door bell ringers who come around and with literature and Scripture verses."

HEAVEN

CHRISTIANS:	JEHOVAH'S WITNESS:
All who are saved by Christ through faith enter one heaven (John 14:1-3; Rev. 21, 22).	The Righteous (those who worked hard enough) have two destinies – Heaven or a Renewed Earth.

HOLY BIBLE

CHRISTIANS:	JEHOVAH'S WITNESS:
Translated from original Greek and Hebrew by experts in these languages who are well known for their linguistic abilities.	New World Translation of the Holy Scriptures: credentials of translators not known. Translations made to support false teachings of Jehovah Witnesses. Example: "Perish" (apollumi) is translated "destroy" or "annihilate," which is not the meaning of the Greek word.

Appendix C

JEHOVAH'S WITNESSES TERMINOLOGY

AWAKE – a *Watchtower* periodical used to introduce Jehovah's Witnesses to the Public and arouse interest in the organization's local meetings.

GOATS – refers to all those outside the Jehovah's Witnesses, those who will be judged by God as in Matthew 25:31-46.

GREAT CROWD – also "sheep," refers to the majority of Jehovah's Witnesses who will not live in heaven but rather will inhabit the restored Paradise Earth after Christ's return.

JEHOVAH – said to be the only correct name for Almighty God.

JEHOVAH'S WITNESSES – a term coined from Isaiah 43:10 in 1931 as the official title of Zion's Watch Tower Tract Society.

KINGDOM HALL – a local meeting place of Jehovah's Witnesses used for instruction of its members.

LITTLE FLOCK – also the "144,000" and the "anointed class," this refers to the elite group of Jehovah's Witnesses who will live in heaven after this life and reign with Christ.

MICHAEL – the archangel who was supposedly Jehovah's first creation and who later became the man Jesus.

NEW WORLD TRANSLATION – the official *Watchtower* Bible, characterized by mistranslations and deliberately designed to support *Watchtower* theology.

THE WATCHTOWER – A Jehovah's Witness' publication for the instruction of its members.

Bibliography

Boa, Kenneth. Cults, *World Religions And The Occult*, Wheaton: Victor Books 1990.

Hoekema, Anthony A. *The Four Major Cults,* Grand Rapids: Eerdmans, 1976.

Larson, Bob. *Larson's New Book of Cults*, Wheaton: Tyndale House, 1982.

Martin, Walter. *The Kingdom of The Cults*, Minneapolis: Bethany House Publishers, 1985.

Jehovah of The Watchtower: A Thorough Expose, Grand Rapids: Baker, 1953.

Rise of The Cults, Santa Anna, CA: Vision House, 1980.

Morey, Robert A. *How To Answer A Jehovah's Witness*, Minneapolis: Bethany House Publishers, 1980.

Ridenour, Fritz. *So What's The Difference?*, Ventura, CA: Regal Books, 1979.

Tucker, Ruth A. *Another Gospel*, Grand Rapids: Zondervan Publishing House, 1989.

Van Baalen, J. K. *The Chaos Of Cults*, Grand Rapids: Eerdmans, 1962.

www.ingramcontent.com/pod-product-compliance
Lightning Source LLC
Chambersburg PA
CBHW070751050426
42449CB00010B/2417